TABLE OF CONTENTS

I.   INTRODUCTION

Federal agencies need talented workers to meet new challenges and complete new missions in the 21st century. Currently, there is an underutilized community of talented individuals who want to work and specifically want to work for the Federal Government. In order to better utilize this untapped pool of talent, on July 26, 2010, President Obama signed Executive Order (EO) 13548 on Increasing Federal Employment of Individuals with Disabilities to mark the 20th anniversary of the signing of the Americans with Disabilities Act (ADA). The EO works to establish the Federal Government as a model employer of individuals with disabilities and to improve efforts to employ workers with disabilities through increased recruitment, hiring, advancement, and retention of these individuals. It requires Federal agencies to increase the hiring of people with disabilities by 100,000 over the next five years.

EO 13548 is not an isolated effort, but works in coordination with EO 13518 on Employment of Veterans in the Federal Government issued on November 9, 2009; Presidential Memorandum on The Presidential POWER Initiative: Protecting Our Workers and Ensuring Reemployment issued on July 19, 2010; and EO 13583 on Establishing a Coordinated Government-wide Initiative to Promote Diversity and Inclusion in the Federal Workforce issued on August 18, 2011, to recruit, hire, and retain workers with disabilities. EO13583 directs Federal departments and agencies to develop and implement a more comprehensive, integrated, and strategic focus on diversity and inclusion as a key component of their human resources strategies. These Executive Orders augment and complement the requirements under Section 501 of the Rehabilitation Act and implementing regulations and Management Directive 715 (MD-715) requiring Federal departments, agencies, and instrumentalities in the executive branch to prepare an affirmative action program for the hiring, placement, and advancement of individuals with disabilities.

Due to the implementation of promising and emerging practices by Federal agencies, more people with disabilities work for the Federal Government now than in the past 20 years. In Fiscal Year (FY) 2011, there were 204,189 employees with disabilities working for the Federal Government, or 11 percent of the Federal workforce. Of these, 18,738 joined the Federal workforce that year, representing 14.7 percent of all new hires.

Despite this progress, there is still a great deal of work to be done. In FY 2011, there were 17,845 people with targeted disabilities working for the Federal Government, or 0.96 percent of the Federal workforce. Of these, 1,122 joined the Federal workforce that year, representing 0.88 percent of new hires. To meet the requirements under EO 13548, there are still approximately 60,000 people with disabilities that need to be hired in FY 2012, FY 2013, and FY 2014.

*Note: The above data is from the Office of Personnel Management (OPM) publication titled *Employment of Individuals with Disabilities in the Federal Executive Branch Report: Data for Fiscal Year (FY) 2011* (http://www.opm.gov/diversityandinclusion/reports/disability/index.aspx) and includes non-seasonal, full-time, permanent employees who self-identified as a person with a disability on Standard Form 256 or 30% or more disabled veterans.

Federal Agency Employment Strategies: A Framework for Disability Inclusion identifies existing, promising, and emerging proactive and dynamic employment strategies and practices for recruiting, hiring, advancing, and retaining qualified individuals with disabilities. This tool can assist Federal agencies in making their workplaces inclusive of and welcoming to people with disabilities.

This tool reflects a combination of legal/regulatory requirements and strategies and practices used by public and private sector employers, including strategies and practices identified in: EO 13548 and guidance provided by OPM; MD-715 and other guidance provided by the Equal Employment Opportunity Commission (EEOC); and plans submitted by 10 Federal agencies under Executive Order 13548 analyzed in a recent report sponsored by the Office of Disability Employment Policy (ODEP), Department of Labor (DOL). Links to useful resources and research are included in an accompanying Resource and Research Compendium. By identifying, adopting, and refining these employment strategies and practices, and making them part of your agency's strategic plan, your agency will benefit from having people with disabilities as part of its vibrant, diverse workforce. These practices are organized into seven action areas:

- **Lead the Way:** Inclusive Agency-Wide Culture
- **Hire (and Keep) the Best:** Personnel Processes
- **Ensure Productivity:** Reasonable Accommodation Procedures
- **Build the Pipeline:** Outreach and Recruitment
- **Communicate:** External and Internal Communication of Agency Policies and Practices
- **Be Tech Savvy:** Accessible Information and Communication Technology
- **Grow Success:** Accountability and Continuous Improvement

II.   LEAD THE WAY: INCLUSIVE AGENCY-WIDE CULTURE

Section 501 of the Rehabilitation Act (Section 501) and Management Directive 715 (MD-715) require each agency to establish an affirmative action program plan for the hiring, placement, and advancement of individuals with disabilities. The plan must provide sufficient assurances, procedures, and demonstrated commitment by agency leadership (agency heads and other senior management officials). MD-715 requires that agency heads issue a written policy statement expressing their commitment to equal employment opportunity and a workplace free of discrimination and harassment. This statement should be issued at the beginning of the agency head's tenure and thereafter on an annual basis and disseminated to all employees. In addition, agency heads and other senior management officials may, at their discretion, issue similar statements when important issues related to equal employment opportunity arise within their agency or when important developments in the law occur.

Executive Order 13548 directs agencies to designate a senior-level official to be accountable for enhancing employment opportunities for individuals with disabilities and targeted disabilities within the agency, consistent with law. This official is to be accountable for developing and implementing the agency's plan, creating recruitment and training programs for employment of individuals with disabilities and targeted disabilities, and coordinating employment counseling to help match the career aspirations of individuals with disabilities to the needs of the agency.

Creating and maintaining a truly diverse and inclusive work environment requires commitment at all levels of your agency. Establishing an inclusive agency-wide culture begins with leadership at the highest levels, including political appointees, personnel in the senior executive service, and their leadership teams. Mid-level managers and supervisors, and particularly human resources staff and other personnel involved in hiring decisions, must also understand the role they play in facilitating an inclusive environment. Finally, communicating the agency's goal of an inclusive and diverse workplace to employees at all levels of the organization and indicating what they can do to help is also extremely important.

Other existing, promising, and emerging strategies for creating and maintaining an inclusive agency-wide culture include the following:

1. Adopting a comprehensive, aggressive, deliberate, continual approach and series of initiatives with leadership as the catalyst, the creation of a strong infrastructure, and successful implementation through senior leadership, commitment, and accountability.

2. Establishing an agency-wide team consisting of executives, managers, and employees with disabilities to support and advance the recruiting, hiring, retention, and promotion of individuals with disabilities. This team may also function as a disability-focused employee resource group (ERG) or affinity group.

3. Making (and publicizing) the business case for employing qualified individuals with disabilities. For example, making the business case includes framing the issue in communication with managers in terms of return on investment, direct and indirect benefits to the agency and to all employees; stressing that enhancing diversity by employing people

with disabilities recognizes changing demographics of the workforce; improving employee engagement, productivity, and reduction of costs; and enhancing retention and advancement.

4. Including disability as part of all of the agency's diversity policies and activities. This includes using the words "disability" and "people with disabilities" in statements defining the agency's diversity policies, inviting disability organizations and people with disabilities to the agency's diversity events, and recognizing that people with disabilities are part of the agency's other diverse communities (including racial and ethnic minority populations, veterans, and the LGBT community).

5. Affirming in policy statements the agency's commitment to equal employment opportunity for people with disabilities and taking affirmative steps to employ, retain, and advance qualified individuals with disabilities at all levels and job positions.

6. Expecting managers to increase their use of special hiring authorities to fill vacancies, including the use of Schedule A.

7. Conducting a summit to secure support, promote dialogue, and explore implementation issues.

8. Encouraging workers with disabilities and other employees to identify barriers, issues, and individual and systemic concerns, without fear of reprisal, and also providing mechanisms such as surveys to allow them to provide this information anonymously.

9. Establishing a universal policy providing workplace flexibility and accommodations for all applicants and employees, with and without disabilities, who can document the need for such flexibility and accommodations, including the use of telework, flexiplace, and flextime options, if appropriate.

10. Implementing work-life programs and initiatives to help employees balance the needs of the workplace with the rest of their lives.

11. Developing emergency management plans that specifically address the needs of employees with disabilities. For example, developing practical guidelines for emergency managers and employees to plan for workplace emergencies addressing issues such as communication about and distribution of the plan, employer responsibilities, first responder responsibilities, employee self-determination, and emergency notification strategies.

III. HIRE (AND KEEP) THE BEST: PERSONNEL PROCESSES

Consistent with Section 501 of the Rehabilitation Act (Section 501) and its implementing regulations and Management Directive 715 (MD-715), it is important for the agency to review its personnel processes, qualification standards, and job descriptions (including the essential functions of each position) to determine whether they facilitate or impede the hiring and advancement of qualified persons with disabilities, including disabled veterans.

To enable and evaluate affirmative action programs to hire, place, or advance individuals with disabilities, the Section 501 implementing regulations and MD-715 specify that the agency may invite applicants for employment to voluntarily indicate whether and to what extent they are individuals with disabilities under specified circumstances. In implementing their employment program plans, Executive Order 13548 directs agencies, to the extent permitted by law, to increase utilization of the Federal Government's Schedule A excepted service hiring authority for persons with disabilities and increase participation of individuals with disabilities in internships, fellowships, and training and mentoring programs.

Personnel processes include the following:

- Self-Identification
- Qualification Standards
- Job Announcements
- Hiring Process, In General
- Special Hiring Authorities
- Special Initiatives for Youth with Disabilities
- Career Development and Advancement
- Retention

A. Self-Identification

Examples of existing, promising, and emerging personnel strategies and practices related to self-identification include the following:

1. Increasing education and awareness of Standard Form (SF) 256-Self-Identification of Disability, the source of Federal disability statistics and informing employees of how self-identification benefits them.

2. Including a description and explanation of the SF 256 Self-Identification of Disability Form at new employee orientation.

3. Distributing a memorandum to human resources (HR) directors providing guidance on effective use of the SF 256-Self-Identification of Disability Form during the on-boarding process.

4. Encouraging existing employees with disabilities to self-identify as a person with a disability, for example sending an annual broadcast message from agency leadership encouraging self-

identification or distributing a memorandum to all employees allowing them to self-identify and explaining benefits and protections.

5. Ensuring that employees can modify/update their SF 256 disability status at any time, e.g., utilize payroll provider to allow employees to update their personal information at anytime.

6. Developing and initiating an aggressive marketing campaign to promote the process of updating profiles.

7. Re-surveying employees on a periodic basis.

B. Qualification Standards

Examples of existing, promising, and emerging personnel strategies and practices relating to qualification standards include the following:

1. Reviewing the agency's eligibility criteria and any agency-specific qualification standards for positions in order to identify and revise criteria and standards that are unnecessarily restrictive and potentially exclude people with disabilities.

2. Assisting hiring managers in the identification of the essential functions of positions to ensure applicants have the requisite knowledge, skills, and abilities to successfully perform them, with or without reasonable accommodations.

3. Reviewing personnel processes and their implementation on an annual basis and making necessary modifications or improvements, when appropriate.

C. Job Announcements

Examples of existing, promising, and emerging personnel strategies and practices relating to job announcements include the following:

1. Indicating in job announcements that the agency encourages applications by qualified individuals with disabilities. The announcement may include the universal access symbol for emphasis as well as communicating the agency's intent to make reasonable accommodations for qualified job applicants and employees with disabilities.

2. Consistent with the President's Hiring Reform initiative, drafting clear, understandable job announcements that explain in plain language the required qualifications and duties of the job and note the availability of reasonable accommodations and contact information for requesting them.

D. Hiring Process, In General

Examples of existing, promising, and emerging personnel strategies and practices relating to the hiring process include the following:

1. Considering applicants with disclosed disabilities for all available positions for which they may be qualified, when the position(s) applied for is unavailable.

2. Implementing a priority consideration model in the hiring process requiring hiring managers to review pre-qualified candidates with disabilities for all grade levels and in various job occupations (inclusive of the Senior Executive Service) in a departmental talent bank prior to the posting of job announcements.

3. In the case that a hiring manager does not select a pre-qualified candidate with a disability, requiring that the hiring manager document for the record the reason for the non-selection.

4. Providing opportunities for practice interviews for job seekers with disabilities referred by community-based organizations who meet qualification standards as a way of identifying potential candidates for current or future job vacancies.

5. Using the Office of Personnel Management (OPM) Shared List of People with Disabilities, a pre-screened database of qualified individuals with disabilities or establishing an agency-wide database of qualified individuals with disabilities.

6. Utilizing a Hiring Manager's Feedback Form for applicant interviews.

7. Ensuring that job offers are not rescinded for inappropriate reasons.

8. Using job fairs as hiring events.

E. Special Hiring Authorities

Examples of existing, promising, and emerging personnel strategies and practices relating to special hiring authorities include the following:

1. Using special hiring authorities, including excepted hiring authorities for individuals with disabilities under Schedule A and rules related to disabled veterans.

2. Developing Schedule A Policies and Procedures.

3. Establishing a talent bank/database to collect resumes and disability certifications from people with disabilities and Schedule A candidates.

4. Creating and using standard language in all job vacancy announcements and making sure they contain information explaining how to apply under Schedule A.

5. Developing standardized training, including training materials for educating key internal and external stakeholders regarding Schedule A and special hiring authorities.

6. Utilizing Schedule A not only for hiring but as a promotion and retention strategy.

7. Establishing a Disability Task Force for Schedule A Hiring and Recruiting.

8. Providing timely input and feedback on Schedule A Policies and Procedures to enhance quality assurance.

9. Developing and implementing methods to track the number and processing of Schedule A applications

10. Providing monthly reports to the Secretary or other agency head that measure progress.

F. Special Initiatives for Youth with Disabilities

Examples of existing, promising, and emerging personnel strategies and practices relating to special initiatives for youth with disabilities include the following:

1. Developing programs for students and recent graduates with disabilities, including building a talent pipeline for youth and young adults with disabilities (transitioning high school students and college students) through mentoring, internships, and work experience programs; summer programs; career days; mock interviews and resume writing (including identifying key words in job descriptions to succeed in electronic keyword searches); youth motivational programs; and job shadowing activities.

2. Establishing a website to encourage mentoring and communication with students and student interns; marketing of website to include recruitment and communication with students who have disabilities.

3. Tracking interns with disabilities included in internship programs.

4. Establishing an accessible centralized one-stop application process for all interns, inclusive of students with disabilities.

5. Establishing a centralized fund to support needed full-time equivalents (FTEs) and funding for payment of student interns with disabilities (under consideration).

G. Career Development and Advancement

Examples of existing, promising, and emerging personnel strategies and practices relating to career development and advancement include the following:

1. Adopting a promotion policy that includes disability among the positive selection factors or that provides priority consideration to qualified employees with disabilities.

2. Determining whether management slots can be set-aside for individuals with disabilities and inform supervisors of the need to nominate employees with disabilities.

3. Adopting an internal targeted recruitment initiative to fill vacancies with individuals with disabilities. This may include a review of employment records to identify qualified employees with disabilities available for promotions or desirable transfers so that their present and potential skills are fully used and developed.

4. Providing training and career enhancement opportunities, including apprenticeship programs, on-the-job training, developmental assignments, job shadowing, mentoring, and tuition reimbursement for current employees with disabilities. These should include strategies to facilitate upward mobility for employees at lower dead-end grades.

5. Providing career enhancement/leadership development opportunities, including reviewing employee development programs to ensure that no barriers exist for people with disabilities.

6. Providing training to leadership, managers, and line staff about new strategies such as workforce flexibility, including customized employment around job tasks (job restructuring, job sharing, and job creation).

7. Ensuring that advertisements for training/workshops in career development include language advising of the provisions of reasonable accommodations.

8. Tracking the number of employees who complete Individual Development Plans and enroll in mentoring programs.

9. Monitoring the composition of participants in training and mentoring programs and tracking and reporting participation rates.

H. Retention

Examples of existing, promising, and emerging personnel strategies and practices relating to retention include the following:

1. Adopting disability management and prevention programs (return-to-work programs).

2. Conducting studies, identifying and implementing methods of collecting feedback on the needs and interests of employees with disabilities, including hosting regular focus groups and allowing for the submission of anonymous surveys.

3. Working with the agency organization for employees with disabilities, to identify specific strategies for improving the retention numbers.

4. Adopting retention plans and strategies based on information obtained from surveys and exit interviews.

5. Developing and disseminating a procedures manual related to the retention of employees with disabilities and targeted disabilities.

6. Developing and implementing a plan to review proposed terminations to ensure disability accommodations were considered, where appropriate.

7. Conducting exit interviews of any persons with a disability leaving Federal employment that include specific questions which will seek to determine if any reason related to the person's disability led to the decision to leave.

8. Analyzing and monitoring terminations of permanent employees and reporting to the Secretary or other agency head and Administration on a quarterly basis.

IV. ENSURE PRODUCTIVITY: REASONABLE ACCOMMODATION PROCEDURES

Some individuals with disabilities may need "reasonable accommodations" in order to perform the essential functions of a job. According to the U.S. Department of Labor's Job Accommodation Network (JAN), data collected suggest that more than half of all accommodations cost nothing. Furthermore, JAN's statistics show that most employers report financial benefits in the form of reduced insurance and training costs and increased productivity.

Under the regulations implementing Section 501 of the Rehabilitation Act and Management Directive 715 (MD-715), an agency must make reasonable accommodation to the known physical or mental limitations of an applicant or employee who is a qualified individual with a disability unless the agency can demonstrate that the accommodation would impose an undue hardship on the operation of its program. In addition, regulations require Federal agencies to include a reasonable accommodation statement on all vacancy announcements. Under Executive Order 13164 and MD-715, each Federal agency must establish effective written procedures for processing requests for reasonable accommodations by employees and applicants with disabilities. Executive Order 13164 specifies the minimum components of effective written procedures.

It is important for agencies to consider the procedures and administrative mechanisms they use to ensure effective and efficient implementation of accommodations. Examples of existing, promising, and emerging strategies and practices relating to reasonable accommodations include the following:

1. Updating reasonable accommodation policies and procedures consistent with the guidelines established by the Equal Employment Opportunity Commission (EEOC), including updates to reflect the Americans with Disabilities (ADA) Amendments Act.

2. Establishing an administrative mechanism for minimizing the cost of an accommodation being assigned to a line manager's budget, such as centralized payments for the costs of providing reasonable accommodations. This is sometimes referred to as a "centralized accommodation fund."

3. Establishing an administrative mechanism or centralized source of expertise (appointing a specific individual and/or establishing an office) for assessing, evaluating, and providing reasonable accommodations (including assistive technology) to ensure the effectiveness and efficiency of the reasonable accommodation process.

4. Consulting with JAN for free, expert, and confidential guidance on workplace accommodations and disability employment issues.

5. Establishing and/or continuing relationships with the Department of Defense's Computer/Electronic Accommodations Program (CAP), the Department of Agriculture's TARGET Center, and/or the Department of Transportation Disability Resource Center.

6. Providing training opportunities to learn about new strategies and devices, such as telework and new assistive technology devices.

7. Creating an online system for tracking accommodations to document their successful use.

8. Assigning a full time director of disability services or workplace supports to coordinate accommodations strategies.

V. BUILD THE PIPELINE: OUTREACH AND RECRUITMENT

Section 501 of the Rehabilitation Act requires all agencies, regardless of size, to have an affirmative action program for individuals with disabilities. Furthermore, agencies with 1,000 or more employees must also have a special recruitment program for individuals with targeted disabilities. In order to meet these responsibilities, agencies often ask: "Where can I find qualified applicants with disabilities?" Agencies have expressed concern that one of the greatest barriers they face regarding the hiring of individuals with disabilities, including veterans with disabilities, is the inability to find qualified candidates. The adoption of effective outreach and recruitment strategies is essential to ensuring that your workforce includes qualified individuals with disabilities, including disabled veterans.

To effectively build a pipeline of qualified applicants with disabilities, your agency will need to develop relationships with a variety of recruitment sources. Such relationships can be formed through formal partnerships (e.g., where agreements are signed that formalize expectations from both parties) or informal interactions (e.g., meetings, exchange of contact information and staffing needs, and ongoing communication regarding job openings and candidates). The investment will be well worth the effort; your agency will not only secure access to talent that it otherwise may have overlooked, but also benefit from other supports that can assist in effectively integrating job candidates with disabilities into your workforce. Some recruitment sources to consider are listed below.

A. Recruitment Sources

1. *Public recruiting sources*, including OPM's Shared List of People with Disabilities, One-Stop Career Centers established under the Workforce Investment Act, State vocational rehabilitation agencies and community rehabilitation programs, State employment agencies, Employment Networks established under the Ticket to Work program, independent living centers established under Title VII of the Rehabilitation Act, and Department of Veterans Affairs Regional Offices.

2. *Educational institutions*, including community colleges, universities, and other institutions of learning and/or training, including those that offer programs for individuals with specific disabilities, such as persons who are blind, deaf, and have learning disabilities. Most college campuses have designated offices for students with disabilities, in addition to career services, which agencies should contact for recruitment purposes.

   In addition, there are several internship programs designed exclusively for students with disabilities, including the Workforce Recruitment Program for College Students with Disabilities (WRP),), Emerging Leaders Internship program, Entry Point! and Project SEARCH.

3. *Non-profit entities and social service* agencies, including labor organizations, organizations of and for individuals with disabilities, and other such entities that may provide referrals, technical assistance, and other advice on proper placement, recruitment, and accommodations.

4. *Private recruiting sources*, including professional organizations, Career Opportunities for Students with Disabilities (COSD), consulting services, and companies with expertise in disability.

B. Outreach and Recruiting Strategies

Existing, promising, and emerging strategies and steps that may be taken to attract and recruit qualified individuals with disabilities include the following:

1. Organizing an agency disability recruitment task force made up of human resources (HR) staff, EEO staff, current employees with disabilities, and managers who have hired persons with disabilities to help the agency establish a network of disability recruitment resources.

2. Adopting special recruitment programs for individuals with targeted disabilities.

3. Appointing a Selective Placement Coordinator to recruit individuals with disabilities who is sufficiently senior to advise management, and is trained in Schedule A and other special hiring authorities, reasonable accommodations, and workforce representation analysis. Responsibilities of the individual may include developing recruitment strategies, establishing contacts with external recruitment sources, and facilitating targeted outreach programs, including through the use of websites and school and employment assistance programs serving persons with disabilities.

4. Holding formal and informal briefing sessions, preferably on agency premises, with representatives from recruiting sources. Integral components of formal briefings include agency tours; explanations of current and future job openings and position descriptions; explanations of the agency's selection process; recruiting literature; and a description of opportunities for formalizing arrangement for referrals of applicants.

5. Establishing formal arrangements for referral of applicants with representatives from recruitment sources, following up with sources, and providing feedback on whether an applicant was interviewed and hired.

6. Implementing a training program (and delivering it to agency employees responsible for recruitment) on how and why to hire individuals with disabilities.

7. Using accessible online applications and recruitment and social networking sites so that job seekers with disabilities can learn about the agency and its hiring initiatives. Such sites can also be used to generate leads with disability-focused organizations nationally and within the geographical area from which the company usually recruits.

8. Joining and actively participating in the Federal Disability Workforce Consortium and eFedLink, a community of practice to advance Federal employment of persons with disabilities.

9. Posting job announcements on accessible web-based "job boards" that specialize in identifying qualified individuals with disabilities (including veterans with disabilities) in disability-related publications and with specific disability service organizations.

10. Participating in career fairs targeting veterans and other candidates with disabilities.

11. Engaging current employees or an employee resource group (ERG) as referral sources and asking if they know individuals with disabilities who would make good job candidates.

12. Including people with disabilities on agency recruitment teams.

13. Building a talent pipeline for youth and young adults with disabilities (transitioning high school students and college students) through mentoring, internships, and work experience programs; summer programs; career days; mock interviews and resume writing (including identifying key words in job descriptions to succeed in electronic keyword searches); youth motivational programs; and job shadowing activities, in addition to requesting that students with disabilities participate in campus recruitment events.

14. Attracting qualified individuals with disabilities not currently in the workforce who have requisite skills, including individuals located through local chapters of organizations of and for individuals with disabilities.

15. Developing specific and targeted strategies for recruiting, hiring, and integrating veterans with disabilities, including wounded returning service members and internal training on these strategies.

16. Designating a coordinator responsible for targeted outreach programs, including websites, schools and employment assistance programs serving persons with disabilities.

17. Developing an electronic mailing list of disability advocacy groups, both nationally and in the local geographic area, and regularly sending e-mail notices to these organizations with all job openings as well as a description of Schedule A authority for people with disabilities and basic instructions on how to apply for a Federal job using it.

18. Using the Internet and social media such as Facebook and Twitter to help recruit individuals with disabilities and raise awareness of the agency as an employer.

C. Assessing Success

Consistent with Management Directive 715 (MD-715), the following existing, promising, and emerging strategies and practices may be used for assessing the success of outreach and recruitment efforts:

1. Reviewing the outreach and recruitment efforts the agency has taken over the previous year to evaluate their effectiveness in identifying and recruiting qualified individuals with disabilities, including individuals with targeted disabilities.

2. Documenting each evaluation, including the criteria used to evaluate the effectiveness of each effort and the agency's conclusion as to whether each effort was effective.

3. Identifying and implementing alternative strategies, if the agency concludes the totality of its efforts were not effective in identifying and recruiting qualified individuals with disabilities.

VI.   COMMUNICATE: EXTERNAL AND INTERNAL COMMUNICATION OF AGENCY POLICIES AND PRACTICES

A. External Communications

To maximize an agency's ability to attract qualified individuals with disabilities, it is important to communicate to the public – and the agency's subcontractors and vendors – the agency's commitment to employing persons with disabilities and the existence of an inclusive and diverse work environment. Examples of existing, promising, and emerging external communication strategies and practices include:

1. Selecting individuals with visible disabilities when employees are pictured in publications and other materials produced by the agency, including job announcements.

2. Sponsoring and participating in job fairs that target job seekers with disabilities, including veterans with disabilities.

3. Informing disability organizations about career days, youth motivation/mentoring programs, and related community activities sponsored by the agency.

4. Sending information about relevant agency policies and priorities to subcontractors, vendors, and suppliers and requesting their support.

5. Communicating with union officials and/or employee representatives to inform them of the agency's policies and seek their cooperation.

6. Using the agency's external/public website to post the agency's:

   - Policy statement regarding inclusion and reasonable accommodation,
   - Special recruitment and hiring initiatives,
   - Targeted internship, mentoring and shadowing programs, and
   - Hiring goals and progress in achieving goals.

B. Internal Communications

Strong external communication strategies and outreach and recruitment initiatives will be more effective if they are accompanied by internal support from supervisory and management personnel and understanding by co-workers who may have limited contact with individuals with disabilities. In addition to the requirement that agency heads issue a written policy statement to demonstrate commitment discussed previously, MD-715 also recognizes that an agency's equal employment opportunity efforts will be most effective if managers and employees are involved in their implementation. Internal communication and other strategies targeting managers, supervisors, and co-workers can foster awareness, acceptance, and support among all levels of staff within the agency.

Examples of existing, promising, and emerging internal communication strategies and practices include the following:

1. Establishing an agency-wide leadership communication network.

2. Establishing a Disability Office that delivers a holistic approach to disability program management by bringing together the operational components of reasonable accommodation, case work, policy, oversight, and education.

3. Establishing a Disability Employment Advisory Council composed of both national and regional representatives such as HR professionals, hiring managers, recruitment coordinators, and employees with disabilities.

4. Supporting a Community of Practice Committee consisting of employees with disabilities and hiring managers to increase the network of disability resources, host focus groups, discuss best practices, and share resources.

5. Developing and implementing an Executive Committee with direct access to the agency head.

6. Establishing a disability employee resource group (ERG) aligned with the agency's diversity program and composed of existing employees with disabilities and employees with family members or friends with disabilities. The purpose of this group would include helping to identify policies and procedures that support a positive work environment for persons with disabilities.

7. Publicizing the agency's commitment in its internal publications (e.g., intranet, employee newsletters/magazines), including publicizing the availability of Schedule A and other special hiring authorities. This includes ensuring that all such information posted is reviewed for compliance with Section 508 of the Rehabilitation Act, and in particular, screen reader compatibility (See "Be Tech Savvy" Section below).

8. Developing a centralized website as a one-stop shop for disability employment information and resources.

9. Using Intranet and e-mail to assist in recruiting individuals with disabilities and to raise awareness.

10. Updating Intranet with appropriate links and information on accelerated hiring process.

11. Posting updated reasonable accommodation procedures on Intranet.

12. Publishing newsletter with useful metrics and resources about agency progress on achieving goals.

13. Conducting special meetings, orientation, and training programs with executive, management, supervisory personnel, union officials and employee representatives for the

purpose of communicating the commitment of the agency and its leadership to foster an inclusive corporate culture and work environment.

14. Including images of employees with disabilities in employee handbooks and other internal publications that feature photographs of employees.

15. Establishing a policy that all managers and supervisors share responsibility for the successful implementation of the agency's inclusion policy and ensuring that they are held accountable through their performance evaluation plans, including how a manager uses Schedule A and other special hiring authorities.

16. As part of the agency's employee assistance program (EAP), adopting disability management and prevention programs (return-to-work programs), with the goal that workers who become injured on the job remain part of the workforce.

17. Adopting recognition and awards program acknowledging individuals responsible for achieving progress and positive outcomes related to disability employment.

18. Including disability-friendly policies regarding internal communications and information dissemination in the agency's policy manual and employee handbook.

VII. BE TECH SAVVY: ACCESSIBLE INFORMATION AND COMMUNICATION TECHNOLOGY

The development, procurement, lease, maintenance, and use of information and communication technology (ICT) are central to the operation of Federal agencies in the 21st century. The Internet has dramatically changed the way that agencies conduct work and communicate with the public, including the manner in which individuals apply for jobs. Further, agency use of the Internet, e-mail, and social media is dramatically changing the way agencies communicate, both internally and externally. Section 508 of the Rehabilitation Act requires agencies to provide Federal employees with disabilities and members of the public access to information and data that is comparable to the access provided to Federal employees without disabilities.

If applicants and employees with disabilities are to fully participate in the workforce, they must have access to and use of information and data that is comparable to the access and use by applicants and employees without disabilities. For example, if an online application system is not accessible to and usable by individuals with disabilities, applicants with disabilities will never "get through the front door" of applying for a job. Once an individual with a disability is on board, if they are not provided with accessible ICT and training, they are limited in their ability to develop skills needed to be productive team members and advance in your agency. A specific commitment by the agency (and all program operating components) to ensure accessible and usable ICT in accordance with Section 508 of the Rehabilitation Act is as essential to facilitating meaningful and effective employment opportunities for individuals with disabilities as structural elements are to ensuring access to buildings and offices.

Existing, promising, and emerging agency practices regarding accessible ICT include the development of comprehensive strategic action plans that include the following areas:

- Leadership and Team Approach
- Needs Assessment and Priorities
- Formal Policies, Practices, and Procedures
- Agency-Wide Infrastructure
- Evaluation and Accountability

A. Leadership and Team Approach

1. Securing leadership at the highest levels of agency leadership, in order to facilitate "buy-in" and establish and sustain organizational commitment.

2. Establishing a network of individuals responsible for implementation (e.g., an accessibility team composed of managers across divisions, including human resources (HR), ICT, procurement, education and training, financial and marketing, and Section 504 and 508 compliance.

3. Making the "business case" for ensuring that technology used by the agency s accessible to the largest possible number of applicants, employees, and customers.

B. Needs Assessments and Priorities

1. Considering all of the ICT used or offered and making a list of those platforms, devices, and applications.

2. Evaluating accessibility by testing of ICT applications with automated accessibility testing tools and by considering the user experience of applicants, employees, and customers.

3. Establishing a process and adopting criteria that can be used for setting priorities.

C. Formal Policies, Practices, and Procedures

1. Adopting specific technical ICT accessibility standards and functional performance criteria regarding software applications and operating systems; Web-based intranet and Internet information applications; telecommunication products; video and multimedia products; self-contained closed products (e.g., copiers and printers); and computers.

2. Adopting accessible online application systems that cover website integration; job posting and distribution tools; application and resume submission; communication between applicants and employer; resume extraction and management; candidate search and selection processes; and communication regarding a job offer or rejection.

D. Agency-Wide Infrastructure

1. Providing outsourcing guidelines to suppliers and partners, including copies of the ICT accessibility guidelines, and ensuring that contracts stipulate suppliers will, where relevant, apply ICT accessibility standards.

2. Establishing clear procurement policies, including a solicitation policy that states ICT should be accessible, indicates which accessibility standards apply, and plans to inspect deliverables based on those standards.

3. Delineating the respective roles and responsibilities of key personnel, including the chief acquisition officer, chief information officer, and chief accessibility technology officer.

4. Conducting training for in-house staff, including program managers, contracting and procurement officers, software developers, web developers, and video-multimedia developers, including IT help desk staff.

5. Deploying accessible ICT throughout the agency by, for example, establishing a mechanism for centralized expertise and/or payment.

E. Evaluation and Accountability

1. Appointing a Chief Accessibility Technology Officer.

2. Notifying managers and employees about the agency's ICT accessibility policy.

3. Involving individuals with disabilities and experts in the development, implementation, and evaluation of policy.

4. Establishing measureable objectives and benchmarks, including checklists, scorecards, and grid-based tracking documents.

5. Designing and implementing data collection and continuous improvement strategies, including tracking and reporting systems and regularly scheduled reporting.

VIII. GROW SUCCESS: ACCOUNTABILITY AND CONTINUOUS IMPROVEMENT

While the adoption of written policies, practices, and procedures are necessary to enhance employment opportunities for qualified individuals with disabilities, the ultimate objective is ensuring their *implementation*. Consistent with Section 501 of the Rehabilitation Act and Management Directive 715 (MD-715), Federal agencies must develop systems for the evaluation of program effectiveness and barrier identification and elimination; ensuring that the agency has adequate data systems for effective analyses of applicant flow, on-board workforce and personnel transaction data, establishing agency-wide objectives and developing and submitting program plans; and preparing accomplishment reports and plan updates for timely submission. In addition, MD-715 states that a model Rehabilitation Act program "will hold managers, supervisors, EEO officials and personnel officers accountable for the effective implementation and management of the agency's program."

Executive Order 13548 expresses the Obama Administration's commitment to increase the number of individuals with disabilities in the Federal workforce by 100,000 over five years. The Executive Order also directs each agency to include in its strategic plan performance targets and numerical goals for employment of individuals with disabilities and sub-goals for employment of individuals with targeted disabilities, and directs each agency to designate a senior-level agency official within the agency responsible for meeting these goals.

Existing, promising, and emerging agency strategies and practices include establishing systems for ensuring accountability and continuous improvement relating to:

- Training and Networking
- Establishing Accountability Measures
- Establishing Accountability, Reporting, and Continuous Improvement Mechanisms
- Designating Responsible Individuals

A. Training and Networking

Often times, "people don't know what they don't know." As is recognized in MD-715, in order to have a model agency Title VII and Rehabilitation Act Program, it is imperative that managers and supervisors be provided with appropriate training and other resources to understand and successfully discharge their duties and responsibilities. Extending such professional development opportunities to employees in all offices, divisions, and departments can also be an effective strategy for demonstrating the agency's firm commitment to equality of opportunity for all employees and applicants. Other examples of existing, promising, and emerging strategies and practices regarding training and networking include:

1. Providing training on disability-related issues, not only to managers, but to all personnel, particularly those involved in the recruitment, hiring, promotion, and retention processes (e.g., understanding legal requirements, disability etiquette and disability awareness, retention and return-to-work strategies, overcoming stereotypes and other attitudinal barriers, reasonable accommodation procedures, targeted hiring programs).

2. Training managers and others on Schedule A and other special hiring authorities.

3. Incorporating training on disability-related issues as a regular and ongoing component of the agency's diversity initiatives.

4. Explaining to managers and supervisors how performance elements included in their performance plans related to the recruitment, hiring, advancement, and retention of persons with disabilities will be assessed, including their use of Schedule A and other special hiring authorities.

5. Actively participating in the Federal Disability Workforce Consortium and eFedLink, a Community of Practice to Advance Federal Employment of Persons with Disabilities; and disability focused conferences like the annual Perspectives on Employment of Persons with Disabilities.

6. Sharing best practices with other Federal agencies through the Office of Personnel Management (OPM), the Chief Human Capital Officer (CHCO) Council and EEO Director Meetings, eFedLink, and the Federal Disability Workforce Consortium.

B. Establishing Accountability Measures

It has been stated that "what's measured gets done." Consistent with MD-715 and Executive Order 13548, specific strategies and practices that your agency can use to measure its progress toward creating an inclusive workplace include establishing annual quantitative goals, objectives, and benchmarks (including for individuals with targeted disabilities) related to the following:

- Outreach and recruitment (including referrals);
- Hiring, retention, and advancement; and
- Sponsored educational, training, recreational, and social activities.

Examples of existing, promising, and emerging practices related to accountability measures include:

1. Focusing on increasing the employment rate of people with disabilities and targeted disabilities, not merely hiring such employees especially in light of the number of individuals with disabilities leaving the workforce; including goals relating both to new hires as well as the permanent workforce.

2. Setting performance targets and numerical goals that will make the agency a model employer. Each agency should have an individual goal and each agency head be held accountable for a proportionate share of the overall goal.

3. Setting goals for hiring or promoting into pay levels and occupations where individuals with reportable and targeted disabilities are not well represented.

4. Tracking and reporting progress closely and re-evaluating hiring and retention goals frequently, on at least quarterly intervals. Monitoring the projections will assist the agency to modify its strategic focus as its hiring climate changes.

5. Updating the agency's Strategic Human Capital Plan to include hiring goals for people with disabilities and requiring the use of hiring and retention data as a critical factor in hiring and workforce succession planning.

C. Establishing Accountability, Reporting, and Continuous Improvement Mechanisms

MD-715 requires that each agency collect, maintain, and analyze applicant flow data and to examine existing recruitment programs and hiring practices to identify and eliminate any barriers to recruiting/hiring individuals with disabilities and, in particular, individuals with targeted disabilities. More specifically, to successfully remove barriers, an agency must do effective barrier analysis, which requires identification of the root cause of the trigger(s), such as a lower than expected participation in the workforce. When the root cause is identified, the agency then needs to develop a comprehensive action plan to eliminate the barrier. The plan should be disseminated to agency managers, who should work in collaboration with the EEO office to implement the plan. The plan should be regularly reviewed and updated to report on progress in eliminating the root cause found, or address modifications that may be needed to the plan if new barriers are found.

It is important that agencies move beyond merely identifying triggers showing the low participation of people with disabilities in the workforce to actually identifying the underlying barrier. Only then can agencies develop the most effective action plans specifically tailored to address that particular barrier. Once the agency identifies its unique barriers, it can incorporate the possible practices discussed below, into an action plan tailored to remove those specific barriers. Only by doing focused barrier analysis can an agency determine which of the following practices are best suited for the agency to address and eliminate an identified barrier.

Accountability and reporting and continuous improvement mechanisms are necessary to ascertain whether current policies, practices, and procedures are effective and whether the agency is making progress in improving employment opportunities for persons with disabilities. Examples of existing, promising, and emerging strategies and practices regarding accountability, reporting, and continuous improvement mechanisms include the following:

1. Reviewing annually all employment-related activities, including:

Job posting, recruitment, advertising, and job application procedures, including testing;

- Hiring, promotion, upgrading, awards of tenure, and layoffs;
- Rates of pay and any other forms of compensation, including fringe benefits;
- Job assignments, job classifications, job descriptions, and seniority lists;
- Sick leave, leaves of absence, and other leave;
- Training, apprenticeships, attendance at professional meetings and conferences; and
- Any other terms, conditions, and privileges of employment.

2. Establishing a system to collect, maintain, and report accurate employment information on disability.

3. Conducting annual self-assessments, including identifying trends and/or issues needing more attention such as:

   - Tracking information related to the provision of reasonable accommodations that could be used to assess the effectiveness of accommodations and the process;
   - Tracking data relating to the representation of individuals with disabilities in the workforce to ascertain trends, including the efficacy of recruitment, hiring, retention, and promotion initiatives; and
   - Establishing a complaint tracking and monitoring system to identify areas needing systemic improvements.

4. Based on reviews and assessments, developing strategic plans that include pro-active steps and the implementation of specific actions necessary to address any noted deficiencies.

5. Providing regularly-scheduled reports to agency leaders and/or other high ranking managers regarding implementation of agency's strategic plans. In reports, identifying completion dates and managers who are accountable and responsible for ensuring that the action items are completed in a timely manner.

6. Seeking input from employees with disabilities regarding implementation of policies and strategic plans using employee surveys, focus groups, and discussions with employee diversity and advisory groups regarding the workplace environment.

D. Designating Responsible Individuals

Designation of authority and responsibility is of central importance to enhancing and securing implementation. Pursuant to MD-715, it is the responsibility of each agency head to take such measures as may be necessary to incorporate the principles of equal opportunity into the agency's organizational structure. MD-715 further states that agencies must maintain a reporting structure that provides the agency's EEO director with regular access to the agency head and other senior management officials for reporting on the effectiveness, efficiency, and legal compliance of the agency's Title VII and Rehabilitation Act programs. In addition, MD-715 indicates that to emphasize the importance of the position, the agency head should be involved in the selection and performance review of the EEO director

EO 13548 also requires each agency to designate a senior-level agency official to be accountable for enhancing employment opportunities for individuals with disabilities and individuals with targeted disabilities within the agency. Related existing, promising, and emerging strategies and practices include:

1. Designating Disability Program Managers who have the same title and grade level as other Special Emphasis Program Managers (with commensurate credentials and duties) and

comparable access to senior management officials and who are fully empowered to implement the agencies' programs.

2. Assigning and defining the scope of responsibility for implementation to specific individuals.

3. Identifying the responsible individual(s) on internal and external communications.

4. Providing top management support (including budgets) and, if appropriate, staff to manage implementation.

5. Explaining to managers and supervisors how performance elements included in their performance plans related to the recruitment, hiring, advancement, and retention of persons with disabilities will be assessed.

RESOURCE AND RESEARCH COMPENDIUM

This Resource and Research Compendium includes a selective list of Federal and State Agency regulatory and policy materials, research studies and reports, and other reports/guidance identifying existing, promising, and emerging practices regarding the recruitment, hiring, retention, and advancement of people with disabilities

EXECUTIVE ORDERS

Executive Order No. 13548 *Increasing Federal Employment of Individuals with Disabilities* (July 26, 2010)

Executive Order No. 13583 *Establishing a Coordinated Government-Wide Initiative to Promote Diversity and Inclusion in the Federal Workforce (August 18, 2011)*

Executive Order No. 13163 *Increasing the Opportunity for Individuals with Disabilities to be Employed in the Federal Government* (July 28, 2000)

Executive Order No. 13164 *Requiring Federal Agencies to Establish Procedures to Facilitate the Provision of Reasonable Accommodation* (July 28, 2000)

Executive Order No. 13078 *Increasing Employment of Adults with Disabilities* (March 13, 1998)

FEDERAL AGENCY WEBSITES/RESOURCES RELATING TO: SECTION 501 OF THE REHABILITATION ACT, EXECUTIVE ORDER 13548, AND SECTION 508 OF THE REHABILITATION ACT

SECTION 501 OF THE REHABILITATION ACT—EQUAL EMPLOYMENT OPPORTUNITY COMMISSION

Section 501 of the Rehabilitation Act and implementing regulations, 29 CFR 1614.203; *Federal Responsibilities under Section 717 of the Title VII and Section 501 of the Rehabilitation Act*, Management Directive 715 (October 1, 2003) and accompanying documents.

Frequently Asked Questions about Management Directive 715 Equal Employment Opportunity Commission

Questions and Answers: Promoting Employment of Individuals with Disabilities in the Federal Workforce Equal Employment Opportunity Commission

Practical Advice for Drafting and Implementing Reasonable Accommodation Procedures under Executive Order 13164 Equal Employment Opportunity Commission, (2005)

EXECUTIVE ORDER 13548 AND TELEWORK

A Toolkit for Federal Agencies on Implementing Executive Order 13548, Office of Disability Employment Policy, U.S. Department of Labor.

Model Strategies for Recruitment and Hiring of People with Disabilities as Required Under Executive Order 13548, Memorandum from John Berry, Director U.S. Office of Personnel Management (November 08, 2010)

eFedLink, *A Community of Practice to Advance Federal Employment of Persons with Disabilities*

Federal Workforce—Practices to Increase the Employment of Individuals with Disabilities, Statement of Yvonne Jones, Director Strategic Issues, U.S. General Accountability Office (February 16, 2011)

Participant-Identified Leading Practices that Could Increase the Employment of Individuals with Disabilities in the Federal Workforce, Highlights of a Forum, General Accountability Office (October 2010)

Improving the Participation Rate of People with Targeted Disabilities in the Federal Work Force, Equal Employment Opportunity Commission (January 2008)

Increasing the Federal Employment of People with Disabilities – Resources for Implementing Executive Order 13548, Memorandum for Heads of Executive Departments and Agencies

A Guide to Telework in the Federal Government, Office of Personnel Management

SECTION 508 OF THE REHABILITATION ACT—GENERAL SERVICES ADMINISTRATION

Section 508 of the Rehabilitation Act and implementing regulations [36 CFR Part 1194] and technical assistance guidance and handbooks; www.buyaccessible.gov See also international accessibility standards applicable to websites. See also Resources for understanding and implementing Section 508

DISABILITY EMPLOYMENT-RELATED RESOURCES—DEPARTMENT OF LABOR

See Office of Disability Employment Policy (ODEP) website. For a comprehensive list of ODEP employment-related links as well as links to other sites, see *Diversifying Your Workforce—A Four Step Reference Guide to Recruiting, Hiring, and Retaining Employees with Disabilities*.

Information regarding customized employment

List of links to websites relating to assistive technology devices and services and accessible information and communication technology (ICT)

29

Information regarding emergency preparedness for people with disabilities

Disability Employment Statistics

Registered Apprenticeship Programs, Employment and Training Administration, Department of Labor

RESOURCE CENTERS—DEPARTMENTS OF DEFENSE, TRANSPORTATION, AND AGRICULTURE

Department of Defense's Computer/Electronic Accommodations Program.

Department of Agriculture's TARGET Center.

Department of Transportation Disability Resource Center.

EMPLOYER RESOURCES—DEPARTMENT OF VETERANS AFFAIRS

The Department of Veterans Affairs Regional Offices locations; See also Employer Resources Section of the National Resource Directory.

RESEARCH PAPERS AND REPORTS

Employment of Individuals with Disabilities in the Federal Executive Branch Report: Data for Fiscal Year (FY) 2011, Office of Personnel Management

Promising and Emerging Practices for Enhancing the Employment of Individuals with Disabilities Included in Plans Submitted by Federal Agencies under Executive Order 13548 (2012)

Business Strategies that Work: A Framework for Disability Inclusion, Office of Disability Employment Policy (2012)

Framework for Designing and Implementing Accessible Information and Communication Technology (ICT) Strategic Plans, Office of Disability Employment Policy (July 20, 2011)

A Technical Assistance Guide for Implementing Online Application Systems that Meet the Needs of Qualified Individuals with Disabilities and Qualified Disabled Veterans, Economic Systems, Inc. (November 2009)

For a comprehensive list of agency regulatory and policy materials, research studies and other policy reports/guidance regarding the recruitment, hiring, retention, and advancement of persons with disabilities and comprehensive examples of best, promising and emerging practices derived from the research studies and policy reports see *Business Strategies that Work* resources.

NON-FEDERAL AGENCY TECHNICAL ASSISTANCE RESOURCES

Job Accommodation Network (JAN), 1-800-526-7234 (voice); 1-877-781-9403 (TTY) Source of expert guidance on workplace accommodations, the ADA and related legislation, and disability employment issues.

Employer Assistance and Resource Network (EARN), 1-855-275-3276 (Voice/TTY) Provides expert advice on hiring and retaining skilled, qualified workers with disabilities.

Disability and Business Technical Assistance Centers. National network of 10 regional ADA Centers that provide services for up-to-date information, referrals, resources, and training on the ADA to businesses, employers, government entities, and individuals with disabilities.

Public sources include One-Stop Career Centers established under the Workforce Investment Act, State vocational rehabilitation agencies and community rehabilitation programs , State employment agencies, Employment Networks established under the Ticket to Work program , and independent living centers established under Title VII of the Rehabilitation Act.

There are several internship programs that are designed exclusively for students with disabilities, including the Workforce Recruitment Program for College Students with Disabilities (WRP), Emerging Leaders program, Entry Point! and Project SEARCH.

U.S. Business Leadership Network, National organization that represents employers using a "business to business" strategy to promote the business imperative of including people with disabilities in the workforce.